DIABETIC COOKBOOK FOR BEGINNERS

THE BEST GUIDE TO PREVENT DISEASE, REVERSE AND MANAGE DIABETES TYPE 1 AND TYPE 2 WITH HEALTHY AND COMFORT RECIPES. START TO LIVING BETTER EFFORTLESS WITH A HEALTHY LIFESTYLE

KAREN L. RAMOS

original author of this work can be in any fashion deemed liable for any hardship or damages that may befall them after undertaking information described herein.

Additionally, the information in the following pages is intended only for informational purposes and should thus be thought of as universal. As befitting its nature, it is presented without assurance regarding its prolonged validity or interim quality. Trademarks that are mentioned are done without written consent and can in no way be considered an endorsement from the trademark holder.

Table Of Contents

Introduction

The Benefits of the Diabetes Meal Prep Meal planning is extremely helpful in many practical ways, but one of its greatest benefits is on a person's health, particularly if it combines healthy balanced food and proper portion control.

Benefit # 1 - It helps improve your general health

Whether or not you have a medical condition, meal planning can help you improve your overall health when the meals provide all the macro and micronutrients your body needs. It also helps you avoid saturated fats and processed sugars, which is what most people would reach for if they're hungry and just want something satisfying.

Benefit # 2 - It ensures that you can eat on time

Preparing your meals in advance helps manage hunger pains. Missing a meal or delaying it can cause your blood sugar level to drop too low, a condition otherwise known as hypoglycemia.

Hypoglycemia can cause shaking, disorientation, and irritability. You may even have a seizure if your blood sugar level gets any lower. Having your meal already prepared ensures that you can always eat on time and, therefore, decrease the risk of low blood glucose.

Benefit # 3 - It lowers your risk of heart disease

Diabetes increases the risk of heart disease. With the help of a dietician, planning your meals can help you reduce this risk. Because meal prep reduces the time you need to spend in the kitchen, you'll have more opportunities to exercise and do other activities that promote a healthier lifestyle.

Benefit # 4 - It lowers your risk of cancer

Diabetes also increases the risk of all forms of cancer. While experts are still unable to identify the exact link between these two conditions, they expect that it has something to do with insulin resistance and obesity. Cancer patients are advised to pursue a healthy lifestyle, which includes eating a balanced diet and getting adequate exercise. Because these activities are also encouraged among diabetics, the risk of cancer is lowered.

Benefit # 5 - It helps you maintain healthy body weight

Again, portion control plays a part in this area. Even if you eat healthy food, overindulging can lead to an unhealthy weight gain, which can make it harder to control your blood sugar level.

If left unchecked, this could lead to high blood sugar levels or hyperglycemia, which can cause various complications that include heart and liver damage as well as the loss of kidney function.

It's important to note that while meal planning can help keep the effects of diabetes under control, you and your dietician still need to conduct a periodic review of its effectiveness and make changes whenever necessary.

How to identify if you have Diabetes

The early signs of diabetes include:

- Hunger and fatigue

When your body consumes food, it converts it into glucose so that the cells can use it for energy. The body needs insulin so that the cells can take in the glucose. Without enough insulin or if the cells are unable to use insulin, the body does not get any energy, making you feel tired as well as hungry all the time.

- Excessive thirst and urination

Usually, a person pees from four to seven times a day. But with people who suffer from diabetes pee a lot more. This also makes you thirsty more frequently.

- Dry mouth and itchy skin

When the body uses fluids to create urine, it has less moisture to keep the mouth and skin from drying.

- Blurry vision

Changes in the body's fluid levels can inflame the

lens of the eyes, making it more difficult for the eyes to focus.

Symptoms of type-2 diabetes include:

- Yeast infections

- Slow-healing wounds

- Pain in the muscles

- Numbness of legs and feet

Symptoms of type-1 diabetes are the following:

- Unexplained weight loss

- Nausea and vomiting

As for gestational diabetes, there are no symptoms. The condition is only determined during prenatal screening.

Breakfast

Spicy Jalapeno Popper Deviled Eggs

Preparation Time: 5 minutes Cooking Time: 5 minutes Servings: 4

Ingredients:

- 4 large whole eggs, hardboiled

- 2 tablespoons Keto-Friendly mayonnaise

- ¼ cup cheddar cheese, grated

- 2 slices bacon, cooked and crumbled

- jalapeno, sliced

Direction:

- Cut eggs in half, remove the yolk and put them in bowl

- Lay egg whites on a platter

- Mix in remaining ingredients and mash them with the egg yolks

- Transfer yolk mix back to the egg whites

- Serve and enjoy!

Nutrition: Calories: 176; Fat: 14g; Carbohydrates: 0.7g; Protein: 10g

Lovely Porridge

Preparation Time: 15 minutes Cooking Time: Nil Servings: 2

Ingredients:

- 2 tablespoons coconut flour
- 2 tablespoons vanilla protein powder
- 3 tablespoons Golden Flaxseed meal
- 1 and 1/2 cups almond milk, unsweetened
- Powdered erythritol

Direction:

- Take a bowl and mix in flaxseed meal, protein powder, coconut flour and mix well
- Add mix to the saucepan (placed over medium heat) Add almond milk and stir, let the mixture thicken
- Add your desired amount of sweetener and serve

Nutrition: Calories: 259; Fat: 13g; Carbohydrates: 5g; Protein: 16g

Salty Macadamia Chocolate Smoothie

Preparation Time: 5 minutes Cooking Time: Nil Servings: 1

Ingredients:

- 2 tablespoons macadamia nuts, salted

- 1/3 cup chocolate whey protein powder, low carb

- 1 cup almond milk, unsweetened

Direction:

- Add the listed ingredients to your blender and blend until you have a smooth mixture

- Chill and enjoy it!

Nutrition: Calories: 165; Fat: 2g; Carbohydrates: 1g; Protein: 12g

Basil and Tomato Baked Eggs

**Preparation Time: 10 minutes Cooking Time: 15 minutes
Servings: 4**

Ingredients:

- garlic clove, minced

- cup canned tomatoes

- ¼ cup fresh basil leaves, roughly chopped

- 1/2 teaspoon chili powder

- 1 tablespoon olive oil

- 4 whole eggs

- Salt and pepper to taste

Direction:

- Preheat your oven to 375 degrees F

- Take a small baking dish and grease with olive oil

- Add garlic, basil, tomatoes chili, olive oil into a dish and stir

- Crackdown eggs into a dish, keeping space between the two

- Sprinkle the whole dish with salt and pepper

- Place in oven and cook for 12 minutes until eggs are set and tomatoes are bubbling

- Serve with basil on top

- Enjoy!

Nutrition: Calories: 235; Fat: 16g; Carbohydrates: 7g; Protein: 14g

Cinnamon and Coconut Porridge

**Preparation Time: 5 minutes Cooking Time: 5 minutes
Servings: 4**

Ingredients:

- 2 cups of water

- cup 36% heavy cream

- 1/2 cup unsweetened dried coconut, shredded

- 2 tablespoons flaxseed meal

- 1 tablespoon butter

- 1 and 1/2 teaspoon stevia

- teaspoon cinnamon

- Salt to taste

- Toppings as blueberries

Direction:

- Add the listed ingredients to a small pot, mix well

- Transfer pot to stove and place it over medium-low heat

- Bring to mix to a slow boil

- Stir well and remove the heat

- Divide the mix into equal servings and let them sit for 10 minutes

- Top with your desired toppings and enjoy!

Nutrition: Calories: 171; Fat: 16g; Carbohydrates: 6g; Protein: 2g

An Omelet of Swiss chard

Preparation Time: 5 minutes Cooking Time: 5 minutes Servings: 4

Ingredients:

- 4 eggs, lightly beaten
- 4 cups Swiss chard, sliced
- 2 tablespoons butter
- 1/2 teaspoon garlic salt
- Fresh pepper

Direction:

- Take a non-stick frying pan and place it over medium-low heat
- Once the butter melts, add Swiss chard and stir cook for 2 minutes
- Pour egg into the pan and gently stir them into Swiss chard
- Season with garlic salt and pepper
- Cook for 2 minutes
- Serve and enjoy!

Nutrition: Calories: 260; Fat: 21g; Carbohydrates: 4g; Protein: 14g

Cheesy Low-Carb Omelet

**Preparation Time: 5 minutes Cooking Time: 5 minutes
Servings: 5**

Ingredients:

- 2 whole eggs
- tablespoon water
- tablespoon butter
- 3 thin slices salami
- 5 fresh basil leaves
- 5 thin slices, fresh ripe tomatoes
- 2 ounces fresh mozzarella cheese
- Salt and pepper as needed

Direction:

- Take a small bowl and whisk in eggs and water
- Take a non-stick Sauté pan and place it over medium heat, add butter and let it melt
- Pour egg mixture and cook for 30 seconds
- Spread salami slices on half of egg mix and top with cheese, tomatoes, basil slices
- Season with salt and pepper according to your taste
- Cook for 2 minutes and fold the egg with the empty half

- Cover and cook on LOW for 1 minute

- Serve and enjoy!

Nutrition: Calories: 451; Fat: 36g; Carbohydrates: 3g; Protein:33g

Yogurt And Kale Smoothie

Servings: 1 Preparation Time: 10 minutes

Ingredients:

- cup whole milk yogurt
- cup baby kale greens
- 1 pack stevia
- 1 tablespoon MCT oil
- tablespoon sunflower seeds
- cup of water

Direction:

- Add listed ingredients to the blender
- Blend until you have a smooth and creamy texture
- Serve chilled and enjoy!

Nutrition: Calories: 329; Fat: 26g; Carbohydrates: 15g; Protein: 11g

Bacon and Chicken Garlic Wrap

**Preparation Time: 15 minutes Cooking Time: 10 minutes
Servings: 4**

Ingredients:

- chicken fillet, cut into small cubes

- 8-9 thin slices bacon, cut to fit cubes   6 garlic cloves, minced

Direction:

- Preheat your oven to 400 degrees F

- Line a baking tray with aluminum foil

- Add minced garlic to a bowl and rub each chicken piece with it

- Wrap bacon piece around each garlic chicken bite

- Secure with toothpick

- Transfer bites to the baking sheet, keeping a little bit of space between them

- Bake for about 15-20 minutes until crispy

- Serve and enjoy!

**Nutrition: Calories: 260; Fat: 19g; Carbohydrates: 5g;
Protein: 22g**

Grilled Chicken Platter

Preparation Time: 5 minutes Cooking Time: 10 minutes Servings: 6

Ingredients:

- 3 large chicken breast, sliced half lengthwise

- 10-ounce spinach, frozen and drained

- 3-ounce mozzarella cheese, part-skim

- 1/2 a cup of roasted red peppers, cut in long strips

- teaspoon of olive oil

- 2 garlic cloves, minced

- Salt and pepper as needed

Direction:

- Preheat your oven to 400 degrees Fahrenheit

- Slice 3 chicken breast lengthwise

- Take a non-stick pan and grease with cooking spray

- Bake for 2-3 minutes each side

- Take another skillet and cook spinach and garlic in oil for 3 minutes

- Place chicken on an oven pan and top with spinach, roasted peppers, and mozzarella

- Bake until the cheese melted

- Enjoy!

Nutrition: Calories: 195; Fat: 7g; Carbohydrates: 3g;

Protein: 30g

Lunch

Chicken, Strawberry, And Avocado Salad

Preparation Time: 10 Minutes Cooking Time: 5 Minutes

Ingredients:

- 1,5 cups chicken (skin removed)

- 1/4 cup almonds

- 2 (5-oz) pkg salad greens or baby Spinach

- (16-oz) pkg strawberries

- avocado

- 1/4 cup green onion

- 1/4 cup lime juice

- 3 tbsp. extra virgin olive oil

- 2 tbsp. honey

- 1/4 tsp. salt

- 1/4 tsp. pepper

Direction:

- Toast almonds until golden and fragrant.

- Mix lime juice, oil, honey, salt, and pepper.

- Mix greens, sliced strawberries, chicken, diced avocado, and sliced green onion and sliced almonds; drizzle with dressing. Toss to coat.

Nutrition: Calories 150 / Protein 15 g / Fat 10 g / Carbs 5 g

Lemon-Thyme Eggs

Preparation Time: 10 Minutes Cooking Time: 5 Minutes Servings: 4

Ingredients:

- 7 large eggs
- 1/4 cup mayonnaise (reduced-fat)
- 2 tsp. lemon juice 1 tsp. Dijon mustard
- tsp. chopped fresh thyme
- 1/8 tsp. cayenne pepper

Direction:

- Bring eggs to a boil.
- Peel and cut each egg in half lengthwise.
- Remove yolks to a bowl.
- Add mayonnaise, lemon juice, mustard, thyme, and cayenne to egg yolks; mash to blend. Fill egg white halves with yolk mixture.
- Chill until ready to serve.

Nutrition: Calories 40 / Protein 10 g / Fat 6 g / Carbs 2 g

Spinach Salad with Bacon

**Preparation Time: 15 Minutes Cooking Time: 0 Minutes
Servings: 4**

Ingredients:

- 8 slices center-cut bacon
- 3 tbsp. extra virgin olive oil
- (5-oz) pkg baby spinach
- 1 tbsp. apple cider vinegar
- 1 tsp. Dijon mustard
- 1/2 tsp. honey
- 1/4 tsp. salt
- 1/2 tsp. pepper

Direction:

- Mix vinegar, mustard, honey, salt and pepper in a bowl.
- Whisk in oil. Place spinach in a serving bowl; drizzle with dressing, and toss to coat.
- Sprinkle with cooked and crumbled bacon.

Nutrition: Calories 110 / Protein 6 g / Fat 2 g / Carbs 1 g

Pea and Collards Soup

Preparation Time: 10 Minutes Cooking Time: 50 Minutes

Servings: 4

Ingredients:

- 1/2 (16-oz) pkg black-eyed peas

- onion

- 2 carrots

- 1,5 cups ham (low-sodium)

- 1 (1-lb) bunch collard greens (trimmed)

- 1 tbsp. extra virgin olive oil

- 2 cloves garlic

- 1/2 tsp. black pepper

- Hot sauce

Direction:

- Cook chopped onion and carrots 10 Minutes.

- Add peas, diced ham, collards, and Minced garlic. Cook 5 Minutes.

- Add broth, 3 cups water, and pepper. Bring to a boil; simmer 35 Minutes, adding water if needed.

Nutrition: Calories 86 / Protein 15 g / Fat 2 g / Carbs 9 g

Spanish Stew

Preparation Time: 10 Minutes Cooking Time: 25 Minutes Servings: 4

Ingredients:

- 1.1/2 (12-oz) pkg smoked chicken sausage links
- (5-oz) pkg baby spinach
- (15-oz) can chickpeas
- 1 (14.5-oz) can tomatoes with basil, garlic, and oregano
- 1/2 tsp. smoked paprika
- 1/2 tsp. cumin
- 3/4 cup onions
- tbsp. extra virgin olive oil

Direction:

- Cook sliced the sausage in hot oil until browned. Remove from pot.
- Add chopped onions; cook until tender.
- Add sausage, drained and rinsed chickpeas, diced tomatoes, paprika, and ground cumin. Cook 15 Minutes.
- Add in spinach; cook 1 to 2 Minutes.

Nutrition: Calories 200 / Protein 10 g / Fat 20 g / Carbs 1 g

Creamy Taco Soup

Preparation Time: 10 Minutes Cooking Time: 20 Minutes Servings: 4

Ingredients:

- 3/4 lb. ground sirloin
- 1/2 (8-oz) cream cheese
- 1/2 onion
- clove garlic
- 1 (10-oz) can tomatoes and green chiles
- 1 (14.5-oz) can beef broth
- 1/4 cup heavy cream
- 1,5 tsp. cumin
- 1/2 tsp. chili powder

Direction:

- Cook beef, chopped onion, and Minced garlic until meat is browned and crumbly; drain and return to pot.
- Add ground cumin, chili powder, and cream cheese cut into small pieces and softened, stirring until cheese is melted.
- Add diced tomatoes, broth, and cream; bring to a boil, and simmer 10 Minutes. Season with pepper and salt to taste.

Preparation Time: 15 Minutes Cooking Time: 5 Minutes Servings: 4

Nutrition: Calories 60 / Protein 3 g / Fat 1 g / Carbs 8 g

Chicken with Caprese Salsa

Ingredients:

- 3/4 lb. boneless, skinless chicken breasts
- 2 big tomatoes
- 1/2 (8-oz) ball fresh mozzarella cheese
- 1/4 cup red onion 2 tbsp. fresh basil
- tbsp. balsamic vinegar
- 2 tbsp. extra virgin olive oil (divided)
- 1/2 tsp. salt (divided)
- 1/4 tsp. pepper (divided)

Direction:

- Sprinkle cut in half lengthwise chicken with 1/4 tsp. salt and 1/8 tsp. pepper.
- Heat 1 tbsp. olive oil, cook chicken 5 Minutes.
- Meanwhile, mix chopped tomatoes, diced cheese, finely chopped onion, chopped basil, vinegar, 1 tbsp. oil, and 1/4 tsp. salt and 1/8 tsp. pepper.
- Spoon salsa over chicken.

Nutrition: Calories 210 / Protein 28 g / Fat 17 g /Carbs 0, 1g

Balsamic-Roasted Broccoli

Preparation Time: 10 Minutes Cooking Time: 15 Minutes Servings: 4

Ingredients:

- lb. broccoli

- tbsp. extra virgin olive oil

- 1 tbsp. balsamic vinegar

- 1 clove garlic

- 1/8 tsp. salt

- Pepper to taste

Direction:

- Preheat oven to 450F.

- Combine broccoli, olive oil, vinegar, Minced garlic, salt, and pepper; toss.

- Spread broccoli on a baking sheet.

- Bake 12 to 15 Minutes.

Nutrition: Calories 27 / Protein 3 g / Fat 0, 3 g / Carbs 4 g

Hearty Beef and Vegetable Soup

Preparation Time: 10 Minutes Cooking Time: 30 Minutes Servings: 4

Ingredients:

- 1/2 lb. lean ground beef
- 2 cups beef broth
- 1,5 tbsp. vegetable oil (divided)
- cup green bell pepper
- 1/2 cup red onion
- 1 cup green cabbage
- 1 cup frozen mixed vegetables
- 1/2 can tomatoes
- 1,5 tsp. Worcestershire sauce
- small bay leaf
- 1,8 tsp. pepper
- 2 tbsp. ketchup

Direction

- Cook beef in 1/2 tbsp. hot oil 2 Minutes.
- Stir in chopped bell pepper and chopped onion; cook 4 Minutes.
- Add chopped cabbage, mixed vegetables, stewed tomatoes,

broth, Worcestershire sauce, bay leaf, and pepper; bring to a boil.

- Reduce heat to medium; cover, and cook 15 Minutes.

- Stir in ketchup and 1 tbsp. oil, and remove from heat. Let stand 10 Minutes.

Nutrition: Calories 170 / Protein 17 g / Fat 8 g / Carbs 3 g

Cauliflower Muffin

**Preparation Time: 15 Minutes Cooking Time: 30 Minutes
Servings: 4**

Ingredients:

- 2,5 cup cauliflower

- 2/3 cup ham

- 2,5 cups of cheese

- 2/3 cup champignon

- 1,5 tbsp. flaxseed

- 3 eggs

- 1/4 tsp. salt

- 1/8 tsp. pepper

Direction:

- Preheat oven to 375 F.

- Put muffin liners in a 12-muffin tin.

- Combine diced cauliflower, ground flaxseed, beaten eggs, cup diced ham, grated cheese, and diced mushrooms, salt, pepper.

- Divide mixture rightly between muffin liners.

- Bake 30 Minutes.

Nutrition: Calories 116 / Protein 10 g / Fat 7 g / Carbs 3 g

- Put 1/4 of grated cheese into ham cup.

- Mix eggs, cream, salt and pepper and divide it into 2 tins.

- Bake in oven 15 Minutes; after baking, sprinkle with green onions.

Nutrition: Calories 180 / Protein 13 g / Fat 13 g / Carbs 2 g

Side Dish

Lemon Garlic Green Beans

Preparation time: 5 minutes Cooking Time: 10 minutes Servings: 6

Ingredients:

- 1 1/2 pounds green beans, trimmed
- 2 tablespoons olive oil
- 1 tablespoon fresh lemon juice
- 2 cloves minced garlic
- Salt and pepper

Direction:

- Fill a large bowl with ice water and set aside.
- Bring a pot of salted water to boil then add the green beans.
- Cook for 3 minutes then drain and immediately place in the ice water.
- Cool the beans completely then drain them well.
- Heat the oil in a large skillet over medium-high heat.
- Add the green beans, tossing to coat, then add the lemon juice, garlic, salt, and pepper.
- Sauté for 3 minutes until the beans are tender-crisp then serve hot.

Nutrition: Calories 75, Total Fat 4.8g, Saturated Fat 0.7g, Total Carbs 8.5g, Net Carbs 4.6g, Protein 2.1g, Sugar 1.7g, Fiber 3.9g, Sodium 7mg

Brown Rice & Lentil Salad

Preparation time: 10 minutes Cooking Time: 10 minutes Servings: 4

Ingredients:

- cup water
- 1/2 cup instant brown rice
- 2 tablespoons olive oil
- 2 tablespoons red wine vinegar
- tablespoon Dijon mustard
- 1 tablespoon minced onion
- 1/2 teaspoon paprika
- Salt and pepper
- (15-ounce) can brown lentils, rinsed and drained
- medium carrot, shredded
- 2 tablespoons fresh chopped parsley

Direction:

- Stir together the water and instant brown rice in a medium saucepan.
- Bring to a boil then simmer for 10 minutes, covered.
- Remove from heat and set aside while you prepare the salad.
- Whisk together the olive oil, vinegar, Dijon mustard, onion,

paprika, salt, and pepper in a medium bowl.

- Toss in the cooked rice, lentils, carrots, and parsley.

- Adjust seasoning to taste then stir well and serve warm.

Nutrition: Calories 145, Total Fat 7.7g, Saturated Fat 1g, Total Carbs 13.1g, Net Carbs 10.9g, Protein 6g, Sugar 1g, Fiber 2.2g, Sodium 57mg

Mashed Butternut Squash

Preparation time: 5 minutes Cooking Time: 25 minutes
Servings: 6

Ingredients:

- 3 pounds whole butternut squash (about 2 medium)
- 2 tablespoons olive oil
- Salt and pepper

Direction:

- Preheat the oven to 400F and line a baking sheet with parchment.
- Cut the squash in half and remove the seeds.
- Cut the squash into cubes and toss with oil then spread on the baking sheet.
- Roast for 25 minutes until tender then place in a food processor.
- Blend smooth then season with salt and pepper to taste.

Nutrition: Calories 90, Total Fat 4.8g, Saturated Fat 0.7g, Total Carbs 12.3g, Net Carbs 10.2g, Protein 1.1g, Sugar 2.3g, Fiber 2.1g, Sodium 4mg

Cilantro Lime Quinoa

Preparation time: 5 minutes Cooking Time: 25 minutes

Servings: 6

Ingredients:

- cup uncooked quinoa
- tablespoon olive oil
- medium yellow onion, diced
- 2 cloves minced garlic
- 1 (4-ounce) can diced green chiles, drained
- 1/2 cups fat-free chicken broth
- ¾ cup fresh chopped cilantro
- 1/2 cup sliced green onion
- 2 tablespoons lime juice
- Salt and pepper

Direction:

- Rinse the quinoa thoroughly in cool water using a fine mesh sieve.
- Heat the oil in a large saucepan over medium heat.
- Add the onion and sauté for 2 minutes then stir in the chile and garlic.
- Cook for 1 minute then stir in the quinoa and chicken broth.

- Bring to a boil then reduce heat and simmer, covered, until the quinoa absorbs the liquid – about 20 to 25 minutes.

- Remove from heat then stir in the cilantro, green onions, and lime juice.

- Season with salt and pepper to taste and serve hot.

Nutrition: Calories 150, Total Fat 4.1g, Saturated Fat 0.5g, Total Carbs 22.5g, Net Carbs 19.8g, Protein 6g, Sugar 1.7g, Fiber 2.7g, Sodium 179mg

Oven-Roasted Veggies

Preparation time: 5 minutes Cooking Time: 25 minutes

Servings: 6

Ingredients:

- pound cauliflower florets

- 1/2 pound broccoli florets

- large yellow onion, cut into chunks

- 1 large red pepper, cored and chopped

- 2 medium carrots, peeled and sliced

- 2 tablespoons olive oil

- 2 tablespoons apple cider vinegar

- Salt and pepper

Direction:

- Preheat the oven to 425F and line a large rimmed baking sheet with parchment.

- Spread the veggies on the baking sheet and drizzle with oil and vinegar.

- Toss well and season with salt and pepper.

- Spread the veggies in a single layer then roast for 20 to 25 minutes, stirring every 10 minutes, until tender.

- Adjust seasoning to taste and serve hot.

Nutrition: Calories 100, Total Fat 5g, Saturated Fat 0.7g, Total Carbs 12.4g, Net Carbs 8.2g, Protein 3.2g, Sugar 5.5g, Fiber 4.2g, Sodium 51mg

Vegetable Rice Pilaf

Preparation time: 5 minutes Cooking Time: 25 minutes

Servings: 6

Ingredients:

- tablespoon olive oil

- 1/2 medium yellow onion, diced

- cup uncooked long-grain brown rice

- 2 cloves minced garlic

- 1/2 teaspoon dried basil

- Salt and pepper

- 2 cups fat-free chicken broth

- cup frozen mixed veggies

Direction:

- Heat the oil in a large skillet over medium heat.

- Add the onion and sauté for 3 minutes until translucent.

- Stir in the rice and cook until lightly toasted.

- Add the garlic, basil, salt, and pepper then stir to combined.

- Stir in the chicken broth then bring to a boil.

- Reduce heat and simmer, covered, for 10 minutes.

- Stir in the frozen veggies then cover and cook for another 10 minutes until heated through. Serve hot.

Nutrition: Calories 90, Total Fat 2.7g, Saturated Fat 0.4g, Total Carbs 12.6g, Net Carbs 10.4g, Protein 3.9g, Sugar 1.5g, Fiber 2.2g, Sodium 143mg

Curry Roasted Cauliflower Florets

**Preparation time: 5 minutes Cooking Time: 25 minutes
Servings: 6**

Ingredients:

• 8 cups cauliflower florets

• 2 tablespoons olive oil

• 1 teaspoon curry powder

• 1/2 teaspoon garlic powder

• Salt and pepper

Direction:

• Preheat the oven to 425F and line a baking sheet with foil.

• Toss the cauliflower with the olive oil and spread on the baking sheet.

• Sprinkle with curry powder, garlic powder, salt, and pepper.

• Roast for 25 minutes or until just tender. Serve hot.

Nutrition: Calories 75, Total Fat 4.9g, Saturated Fat 0.7g, Total Carbs 7.4g, Net Carbs 3.9g, Protein 2.7g, Sugar 3.3g, Fiber 3.5g, Sodium 40mg

Mushroom Barley Risotto

Preparation time: 5 minutes Cooking Time: 25 minutes Servings: 8

Ingredients:

- 4 cups fat-free beef broth
- 2 tablespoons olive oil
- small onion, diced well
- 2 cloves minced garlic
- 8 ounces thinly sliced mushrooms
- ¼ tsp. dried thyme
- Salt and pepper
- cup pearled barley
- 1/2 cup dry white wine

Direction:

- Heat the beef broth in a medium saucepan and keep it warm.
- Heat the oil in a large, deep skillet over medium heat.
- Add the onions and garlic and sauté for 2 minutes then stir in the mushrooms and thyme.
- Season with salt and pepper and sauté for 2 minutes more.
- Add the barley and sauté for 1 minute then pour in the wine.
- Ladle about 1/2 cup of beef broth into the skillet and stir well to combine.

- Cook until most of the broth has been absorbed then add another ladle.

- Repeat until you have used all of the broth and the barley is cooked to al dente.

- Adjust seasoning to taste with salt and pepper and serve hot.

Nutrition: Calories 155, Total Fat 4.4g, Saturated Fat 0.6g, Total Carbs 21.9g, Net Carbs 17.5g, Protein 5.5g, Sugar 1.2g, Fiber 4.4g, Sodium 455mg

Braised Summer Squash

**Preparation time: 10 minutes Cooking Time: 20 minutes
Servings: 6**

Ingredients:

- 3 tablespoons olive oil

- 3 cloves minced garlic

- ¼ teaspoon crushed red pepper flakes

- 1 pound summer squash, sliced

- 1 pound zucchini, sliced

- teaspoon dried oregano

- Salt and pepper

Direction:

- Heat the oil in a large skillet over medium heat.

- Add the garlic and crushed red pepper and cook for 2 minutes.

- Add the summer squash and zucchini and cook for 15 minutes, stirring often, until just tender.

- Stir in the oregano then season with salt and pepper to taste. serve hot.

Nutrition: Calories 90, Total Fat 7.4g, Saturated Fat 1.1g, Total Carbs 6.2g, Net Carbs 4.4g, Protein 1.8g, Sugar 4g, Fiber 1.8g, Sodium 10mg

Parsley Tabbouleh

Preparation time: 5 minutes Cooking Time: 25 minutes
Servings: 6

Ingredients:

- cup water
- 1/2 cup bulgur
- ¼ cup fresh lemon juice
- 2 tablespoons olive oil
- 2 cloves minced garlic
- Salt and pepper
- 2 cups fresh chopped parsley
- 2 medium tomatoes, died
- small cucumber, diced
- ¼ cup fresh chopped mint

Direction:

- Bring the water and bulgur to a boil in a small saucepan then remove from heat.
- Cover and let stand until the water is fully absorbed, about 25 minutes.
- Meanwhile, whisk together the lemon juice, olive oil, garlic, salt, and pepper in a medium bowl.

- Toss in the cooked bulgur along with the parsley, tomatoes, cucumber, and mint.

- Season with salt and pepper to taste and serve.

Nutrition: Calories 110, Total Fat 5.3g, Saturated Fat 0.9g, Total Carbs 14.4g, Net Carbs 10.5g, Protein 3g, Sugar 2.4g, Fiber 3.9g, Sodium 21mg

SOUPS AND STEWS

Kidney Bean Stew

Preparation time: 15 minutes ,Cooking time: 15 minutes
Servings: 2

Ingredients:

• 1lb cooked kidney beans

• 1 cup tomato passata

• 1 cup low sodium beef broth

• 3tbsp Italian herbs

Direction:

• Mix all the ingredients in your Instant Pot.

• Cook on Stew for 15 minutes.

• Release the pressure naturally.

Nutrition: Calories: 270; Carbs: 16; Sugar: 3; Fat: 10; Protein: 23; GL: 8

Cabbage Soup

Preparation time: 15 minutes, Cooking time: 35 minutes
Servings: 2

Ingredients:

- 1lb shredded cabbage

- cup low sodium vegetable broth

- 1 shredded onion   2tbsp mixed herbs

- 1tbsp black pepper

Direction:

- Mix all the ingredients in your Instant Pot.

- Cook on Stew for 35 minutes.

- Release the pressure naturally.

Nutrition: Calories: 60; Carbs: 2; Sugar: 0; Fat: 2; Protein: 4; GL: 1

Pumpkin Spice Soup

Preparation time: 10 minutes Cooking time: 35 minutes

Servings: 2

Ingredients:

- 1lb cubed pumpkin

- 1 cup low sodium vegetable broth

- 2tbsp mixed spice

Direction:

- Mix all the ingredients in your Instant Pot.

- Cook on Stew for 35 minutes.

- Release the pressure naturally.

- Blend the soup.

Nutrition: Calories: 100; Carbs: 7; Sugar: 1; Fat: 2; Protein: 3; GL: 1

Cream of Tomato Soup

Preparation time: 15 minutes , Cooking time: 15 minutes
Servings: 2

Ingredients:

- 1lb fresh tomatoes, chopped
- 1.5 cups low sodium tomato puree
- 1tbsp black pepper

Direction:

- Mix all the ingredients in your Instant Pot.
- Cook on Stew for 15 minutes.
- Release the pressure naturally.
- Blend.

Nutrition: Calories: 20; Carbs: 2; Sugar: 1; Fat: 0; Protein: 3; GL: 1

Shiitake Soup

Preparation time: 15 minutes , Cooking time: 35 minutes

Servings: 2

Ingredients:

- cup shiitake mushrooms

- 1 cup diced vegetables

- 1 cup low sodium vegetable broth

- 2tbsp 5 spice seasoning

Direction:

- Mix all the ingredients in your Instant Pot.

- Cook on Stew for 35 minutes.

- Release the pressure naturally.

Nutrition: Calories: 70; Carbs: 5; Sugar: 1; Fat: 2; Protein: 2; GL: 1

Spicy Pepper Soup

Preparation time: 15 minutes , Cooking time: 15 minutes
Servings: 2

Ingredients:

- 1lb chopped mixed sweet peppers

- 1 cup low sodium vegetable broth

- 3tbsp chopped chili peppers

- 1tbsp black pepper

Direction:

- Mix all the ingredients in your Instant Pot.

- Cook on Stew for 15 minutes.

- Release the pressure naturally. Blend.

Nutrition: Calories: 100; Carbs: 11; Sugar: 4; Fat: 2; Protein: 3; GL: 6

Zoodle Won-Ton Soup

Preparation time: 15 minutes , Cooking time: 5 minutes
Servings: 2

Ingredients:

• 1lb spiralized zucchini

• 1 pack unfried won-tons

• 1 cup low sodium beef broth

• 2tbsp soy sauce

Direction:

• Mix all the ingredients in your Instant Pot.

• Cook on Stew for 5 minutes.

• Release the pressure naturally.

Nutrition: Calories: 300; Carbs: 6; Sugar: 1; Fat: 9; Protein: 43; GL: 2

Broccoli Stilton Soup

Preparation time: 15 minutes , Cooking time: 35 minutes
Servings: 2

Ingredients:

- 1lb chopped broccoli

- 0.5lb chopped vegetables

- 1 cup low sodium vegetable broth

- cup Stilton

Direction:

- Mix all the ingredients in your Instant Pot.

- Cook on Stew for 35 minutes.

- Release the pressure naturally.

- Blend the soup.

Nutrition: Calories: 280; Carbs: 9; Sugar: 2; Fat: 22; Protein: 13; GL: 4

Lamb Stew Recipe 2

Preparation time: 15 minutes , Cooking time: 35 minutes

Servings: 2

Ingredients:

- 1lb diced lamb shoulder
- 1lb chopped winter vegetables
- 1 cup low sodium vegetable broth
- 1tbsp yeast extract
- 1tbsp star anise spice mix

Direction:

- Mix all the ingredients in your Instant Pot.
- Cook on Stew for 35 minutes.
- Release the pressure naturally.

Nutrition: Calories: 320; Carbs: 10; Sugar: 2; Fat: 8; Protein: 42; GL: 3

Irish Stew

Preparation time: 15 minutes , Cooking time: 35 minutes
Servings: 2

Ingredients:

- 1.5lb diced lamb shoulder
- 1lb chopped vegetables
- 1 cup low sodium beef broth
- 3 minced onions
- 1tbsp ghee

Direction:

- Mix all the ingredients in your Instant Pot.
- Cook on Stew for 35 minutes.
- Release the pressure naturally.

Nutrition: Calories: 330; Carbs: 9; Sugar: 2; Fat: 12; Protein: 49; GL: 3

Dinner

Creamed Spinach

Preparation Time: 5 Minutes **Cooking Time:** 10 Minutes
Servings: 4

Ingredients:

- 3 tbsp. Butter
- ¼ tsp. Black Pepper
- 4 cloves of Garlic, minced
- ¼ tsp. Sea Salt
- 10 oz. Baby Spinach, chopped
- tsp. Italian Seasoning
- 1/2 cup Heavy Cream
- 3 oz. Cream Cheese

Direction:

- Melt butter in a large sauté pan over medium heat.
- Once the butter has melted, spoon in the garlic and sauté for 30 seconds or until aromatic.
- Spoon in the spinach and cook for 3 to 4 minutes or until wilted.
- Add all the remaining ingredients to it and continuously stir

until the cream cheese melts and the mixture gets thickened.

• Serve hot

Nutrition: Calories – 274kL; Fat – 27g; Carbs – 4g; Protein – 4g; Sodium – 114mg

Stuffed Mushrooms

Preparation Time: 10 Minutes Cooking Time: 20 Minutes
Servings: 4

Ingredients:

• 4 Portobello Mushrooms, large

• 1/2 cup Mozzarella Cheese, shredded

• 1/2 cup Marinara, low-sugar

• Olive Oil Spray

Direction:

• Preheat the oven to 375 F.

• Take out the dark gills from the mushrooms with the help of a spoon.

• Keep the mushroom stem upside down and spoon it with two tablespoons of marinara sauce and mozzarella cheese.

• Bake for 18 minutes or until the cheese is bubbly.

Nutrition: Calories – 113kL; Fat – 6g; Carbs – 4g; Protein – 7g; Sodium – 14mg

Vegetable Soup

Preparation Time: 10 Minutes Cooking Time: 30 Minutes
Servings: 5

Ingredients:

• 8 cups Vegetable Broth

• 2 tbsp. Olive Oil

• tbsp. Italian Seasoning

• Onion, large & diced

• 2 Bay Leaves, dried

• 2 Bell Pepper, large & diced

• Sea Salt & Black Pepper, as needed

• 4 cloves of Garlic, minced

• 28 oz. Tomatoes, diced

• Cauliflower head, medium & torn into florets

• 2 cups Green Beans, trimmed & chopped

Direction:

• Heat oil in a Dutch oven over medium heat.

• Once the oil becomes hot, stir in the onions and pepper.

• Cook for 10 minutes or until the onion is softened and browned.

• Spoon in the garlic and sauté for a minute or until fragrant.

- Add all the remaining ingredients to it. Mix until everything comes together.

- Bring the mixture to a boil. Lower the heat and cook for further 20 minutes or until the vegetables have softened.

- Serve hot.

Nutrition: Calories – 79kL; Fat – 2g; Carbs – 8g; Protein – 2g; Sodium – 187mg

Misto Quente

Preparation time: 5 minutes Cooking time: 10 minutes Servings: 4

Ingredients:

- 4 slices of bread without shell
- 4 slices of turkey breast
- 4 slices of cheese
- 2 tbsp. cream cheese
- 2 spoons of butter

Direction:

- Preheat the air fryer. Set the timer of 5 minutes and the temperature to 200C.
- Pass the butter on one side of the slice of bread, and on the other side of the slice, the cream cheese.
- Mount the sandwiches placing two slices of turkey breast and two slices cheese between the breads, with the cream cheese inside and the side with butter.
- Place the sandwiches in the basket of the air fryer. Set the timer of the air fryer for 5 minutes and press the power button.

Nutrition: Calories: 340 Fat: 15g Carbs: 32g Protein: 15g

Sugar: 0g Cholesterol: 0mg

Garlic Bread

Preparation time: 10 minutes Cooking time: 15 minutes Servings: 4-5

Ingredients:

- Garlic Bread

- 2 stale French rolls

- 4 tbsp. crushed or crumpled garlic

- 1 cup of mayonnaise

- Powdered grated Parmesan

- tbsp. olive oil

Direction :

- Preheat the air fryer. Set the time of 5 minutes and the temperature to 2000C.

- Mix mayonnaise with garlic and set aside.

- Cut the baguettes into slices, but without separating them completely.

- Fill the cavities of equals. Brush with olive oil and sprinkle with grated cheese.

- Place in the basket of the air fryer. Set the timer to 10 minutes, adjust the temperature to 1800C and press the power button.

Nutrition: Calories: 340 Fat: 15g Carbs: 32g Protein: 15g Sugar: 0g Cholesterol: 0mg

Bruschetta

Preparation time: 5 minutes|Cooking time: 10 minutes
Servings: 2

Ingredients:

- 4 slices of Italian bread
- cup chopped tomato tea
- 1 cup grated mozzarella tea
- Olive oil
- Oregano, salt, and pepper
- 4 fresh basil leaves

Direction:

- Preheat the air fryer. Set the timer of 5 minutes and the temperature to 2000C.
- Sprinkle the slices of Italian bread with olive oil. Divide the chopped tomatoes and mozzarella between the slices. Season with salt, pepper, and oregano.
- Put oil in the filling. Place a basil leaf on top of each slice.
- Put the bruschetta in the basket of the air fryer being careful not to spill the filling. Set the timer of 5 minutes, set the temperature to 180C, and press the power button.
- Transfer the bruschetta to a plate and serve.

Nutrition: Calories: 434 Fat: 14g Carbohydrates: 63g Protein: 11g Sugar: 8g Cholesterol: 0mg

Cream Buns with Strawberries

Preparation time: 10 minutes Cooking time: 12 minutes
Servings: 6

Ingredients:

- 240g all-purpose flour

- 50g granulated sugar

- 8g baking powder

- 1g of salt

- 85g chopped cold butter

- 84g chopped fresh strawberries

- 120 ml whipping cream

- 2 large eggs

- 10 ml vanilla extract

- 5 ml of water

Direction:

- Sift flour, sugar, baking powder and salt in a large bowl. Put the butter with the flour with the use of a blender or your hands until the mixture resembles thick crumbs.

- Mix the strawberries in the flour mixture. Set aside for the mixture to stand. Beat the whipping cream, 1 egg and the vanilla extract in a separate bowl.

- Put the cream mixture in the flour mixture until they are

homogeneous, and then spread the mixture to a thickness of 38 mm.

- Use a round cookie cutter to cut the buns. Spread the buns with a combination of egg and water. Set aside

- Preheat the air fryer, set it to 180C.

- Place baking paper in the preheated inner basket.

- Place the buns on top of the baking paper and cook for 12 minutes at 180C, until golden brown.

Nutrition: Calories: 150Fat: 14g Carbs: 3g Protein: 11g Sugar: 8g Cholesterol: 0mg

Blueberry Buns

Preparation time: 10 minutes Cooking time: 12 minutes Servings: 6

Ingredients:

- 240g all-purpose flour
- 50g granulated sugar
- 8g baking powder
- 2g of salt
- 85g chopped cold butter
- 85g of fresh blueberries
- 3g grated fresh ginger
- 113 ml whipping cream
- 2 large eggs
- 4 ml vanilla extract
- 5 ml of water

Direction:

- Put sugar, flour, baking powder and salt in a large bowl.
- Put the butter with the flour using a blender or your hands until the mixture resembles thick crumbs.
- Mix the blueberries and ginger in the flour mixture and set aside

- Mix the whipping cream, 1 egg and the vanilla extract in a different container.

- Put the cream mixture with the flour mixture until combined.

- Shape the dough until it reaches a thickness of approximately 38 mm and cut it into eighths.

- Spread the buns with a combination of egg and water. Set aside Preheat the air fryer set it to 180C.

- Place baking paper in the preheated inner basket and place the buns on top of the paper. Cook for 12 minutes at 180C, until golden brown

Nutrition: Calories: 105 Fat: 1.64g Carbs: 20.09g Protein: 2.43g Sugar: 2.1g Cholesterol: 0mg

Cauliflower Potato Mash

Preparation Time: 30 minutes Servings: 4 Cooking Time: 5 minutes

Ingredients:

- 2 cups potatoes, peeled and cubed
- 2 tbsp. butter
- ¼ cup milk
- 10 oz. cauliflower florets
- ¾ tsp. salt

Direction:

- Add water to the saucepan and bring to boil.
- Reduce heat and simmer for 10 minutes.
- Drain vegetables well. Transfer vegetables, butter, milk, and salt in a blender and blend until smooth.

Nutrition: Calories 128 Fat 6.2 g, Sugar 3.3 g, Protein 3.2 g, Cholesterol 17 mg

French toast in Sticks

Preparation time: 5 minutes Cooking time: 10 minutes Servings: 4

Ingredients:

- 4 slices of white bread, 38 mm thick, preferably hard
- 2 eggs
- 60 ml of milk
- 15 ml maple sauce
- 2 ml vanilla extract
- Nonstick Spray Oil
- 38g of sugar
- 3ground cinnamon
- Maple syrup, to serve
- Sugar to sprinkle

Direction:

- Cut each slice of bread into thirds making 12 pieces. Place sideways
- Beat the eggs, milk, maple syrup and vanilla.
- Preheat the air fryer, set it to 175C.
- Dip the sliced bread in the egg mixture and place it in the preheated air fryer. Sprinkle French toast generously with oil

spray.

- Cook French toast for 10 minutes at 175C. Turn the toast halfway through cooking.

- Mix the sugar and cinnamon in a bowl.

- Cover the French toast with the sugar and cinnamon mixture when you have finished cooking.

- Serve with Maple syrup and sprinkle with powdered sugar

Nutrition:: Calories 128, Fat 6.2 g, Carbs 16.3 g, Sugar 3.3 g, Protein 3.2 g Cholesterol 17 mg

Dark Chocolate Cake

Preparation Time: 10 minutes, Cooking time: 3 hours

Servings: 10

Ingredients:

- cup almond flour

- 3 eggs

- 2 tablespoons almond flour

- 1/4 teaspoon salt

- 1/2 cup Swerve Granular

- 3/4 teaspoon vanilla extract

- 2/3 cup almond milk, unsweetened

- 1/2 cup cocoa powder

- 6 tablespoons butter, melted

- 1/2 teaspoon baking powder

- 3 tablespoon unflavored whey protein powder or egg white protein powder

- 1/3 cup sugar-free chocolate chips, optional

Direction:

- Grease the slow cooker well.

- Whisk the almond flour together with cocoa powder, sweetener, whey protein powder, salt and baking powder in a bowl. Then stir in butter along with almond milk, eggs and the vanilla extract until well combined, and then stir in the chocolate chips if desired.

- When done, pour into the slow cooker. Allow to cook for 2-2 1/2 hours on low.

- When through, turn off the slow cooker and let the cake cool for about 20-30 minutes.

- When cooled, cut the cake into pieces and serve warm with lightly sweetened whipped cream. Enjoy!

Nutrition:205 calories; 17 g fat; 8.4 g total carbs; 12 g protein

Lemon Custard

Preparation Time: 10 minutes, Cooking time: 3 hours

Servings: 4

Ingredients:

- 2 cups whipping cream or coconut cream

- 5 egg yolks

- tablespoon lemon zest

- 1 teaspoon vanilla extract

- 1/4 cup fresh lemon juice, squeezed

- 1/2 teaspoon liquid stevia

- Lightly sweetened whipped cream

Direction:

- Whisk egg yolks together with lemon zest, liquid stevia, lemon zest and vanilla in a bowl, and then whisk in heavy cream.

- Divide the mixture among 4 small jars or ramekins.

- To the bottom of a slow cooker add a rack, and then add ramekins on top of the rack and add enough water to cover half of ramekins.

- Close the lid and cook for 3 hours on low. Remove ramekins.

- Let cool to room temperature, and then place into the refrigerator to cool completely for about 3 hours.

- When through, top with the whipped cream and serve.

Enjoy!

Nutrition:319 calories; 30 g fat; 3 g total carbs; 7 g protein

Chocolate & Raspberry Ice Cream

Preparation Time: 12 hours and 20 minutes Cooking Time: 0 minutes Servings: 8

Ingredients:

- ¼ cup almond milk

- 2 egg yolks

- 2 tablespoons cornstarch

- ¼ cup honey

- ¼ teaspoon almond extract

- ⅛ teaspoon salt

- 1 cup fresh raspberries

- 2 oz. dark chocolate, chopped

- ¼ cup almonds, slivered and toasted

Direction:

- Mix almond milk, egg yolks, cornstarch and honey in a bowl. Pour into a saucepan over medium heat.

- Cook for 8 minutes. Strain through a sieve. Stir in salt and almond extract.

- Chill for 8 hours.

- Put into an ice cream maker.

- Follow manufacturer's directions.

- Stir in the rest of the ingredients. Freeze for 4 hours.

Nutrition: Calories 142 Total Fat 7 g Saturated Fat 2 g Cholesterol 70 mg Sodium 87 mg Total Carbohydrate 18 g Dietary Fiber 2 g Total Sugars 13 g Protein 3 g Potassium 150 mg

Choco Banana Bites

Preparation Time: 2 hours and 5 minutes Cooking Time: 5 minutes Servings: 4

Ingredients:

- 2 bananas, sliced into rounds
- ¼ cup dark chocolate cubes

Direction:

- Melt chocolate in the microwave or in a saucepan over medium heat.
- Coat each banana slice with melted chocolate.
- Place on a metal pan. Freeze for 2 hours.

Nutrition: Calories 102 Total Fat 3 g Saturated Fat 2 g Cholesterol 0 mg Sodium 4 mg Total Carbohydrate 20 g Dietary Fiber 2 g Total Sugars 13 g Protein 1 g Potassium 211 mg

Blueberries with Yogurt

Preparation Time: 5 minutes Cooking Time: 0 minute

Serving: 1

Ingredients:

- 1 cup nonfat Greek yogurt

- ¼ cup blueberries

- ¼ cup almonds

Direction:

- Add yogurt and blueberries in a food processor.

- Pulse until smooth. Top with almonds before serving.

Nutrition: Calories 154 Total Fat 1 g Saturated Fat 0 g Cholesterol 11 mg Sodium 81 mg Total Carbohydrate 13 g Dietary Fiber 1 g Total Sugars 11 g Protein 23 g Potassium 346 mg

Roasted Mangoes

Preparation Time: 5 minutes Cooking Time: 10 minutes
Servings: 4

Ingredients:

- 2 mangoes, peeled and sliced into cubes

- 2 tablespoons coconut flakes

- 2 teaspoons crystallized ginger, chopped

- 2 teaspoons orange zest

Direction:

- Preheat your oven to 350 degrees F. Put the mango cubes in custard cups.

- Top with the ginger and orange zest. Bake in the oven for 10 minutes.

Nutrition: Calories 89 Total Fat 2 g Saturated Fat 1 g Cholesterol 0 mg Sodium 14 mg Total Carbohydrate 20 g Dietary Fiber 2 g Total Sugars 17 g Protein 1 g Potassium 177 mg

Figs with Yogurt

Preparation Time: 8 hours and 5 minutes Cooking Time: 0 minutes Servings: 2

Ingredients:

- 8 oz. low fat yogurt ½ teaspoon vanilla

- 2 figs, sliced

- tablespoon walnuts, toasted and chopped

- Lemon zest

Direction:

- Refrigerate yogurt in a bowl for 8 hours.

- After 8 hours, take it out of the refrigerator and stir in yogurt and vanilla.

- Stir in the figs.

- Sprinkle walnuts and lemon zest on top before serving.

Nutrition: Calories 157 Total Fat 4 g Saturated Fat 1 g Cholesterol 7 mg Sodium 80 mg Total Carbohydrate 24 g Dietary Fiber 2 g Total Sugars 1 g Protein 7 g Potassium 557mg

Grilled Peaches

Preparation Time: 5 minutes Cooking Time: 3 minutes Servings: 6

Ingredients:

- cup balsamic vinegar

- ⅛ teaspoon ground cinnamon

- tablespoon honey

- 3 peaches, pitted and sliced in half

- 2 teaspoons olive oil

- 6 gingersnaps, crushed

Direction:

- Pour the vinegar into a saucepan. Bring it to a boil. Lower heat and simmer for 10 minutes.

- Remove from the stove. Stir in cinnamon and honey.

- Coat the peaches with oil. Grill peaches for 2 to 3 minutes.

- Drizzle each one with syrup. Top with the gingersnaps.

Nutrition:: Calories 135 Total Fat 3 g Saturated Fat 1 g Cholesterol 0 mg Sodium 42 mg Total Carbohydrate 25 g Dietary Fiber 2 g Total Sugars 18 g Protein 1 g Potassium 251 mg

Fruit Salad

Preparation Time: 5 minutes Cooking Time: 0 minute

Servings: 6

Ingredients:

- 8 oz. light cream cheese

- 6 oz. Greek yogurt

- tablespoon honey

- teaspoon orange zest

- 1 teaspoon lemon zest

- 1 orange, sliced into sections

- 3 kiwi fruit, peeled and sliced 1 mango, cubed

- cup blueberries

Direction:

- Beat cream cheese using an electric mixer.

- Add yogurt and honey. Beat until smooth.

- Stir in the orange and lemon zest.

- Toss the fruits to mix.

- Divide in glass jars. Top with the cream cheese mixture.

Nutrition: Calories 131 Total Fat 3 g Saturated Fat 2 g Cholesterol 9 mg Sodium 102 mg Total Carbohydrate 23 g Dietary Fiber 3 g Total Sugars 18 g Protein 5 g Potassium 234 mg

Strawberry & Watermelon Pops

Preparation Time: 6 hours and 10 minutes Cooking Time: 0 minutes Servings: 6

Ingredients:

- ¾ cup strawberries, sliced

- 2 cups watermelon, cubed

- ¼ cup lime juice

- 2 tablespoons brown sugar

- ⅛ teaspoon salt

Direction:

- Put the strawberries inside popsicle molds. In a blender, pulse the rest of the ingredients until well mixed.

- Pour the puree into a sieve before pouring into the molds. Freeze for 6 hours.

Nutrition: Calories 57 Total Fat 0 g Saturated Fat 0 g Cholesterol 0 mg Sodium 180 mg Total Carbohydrate 14 g Dietary Fiber 2 g Total Sugars 11 g Protein 1 g Potassium 180 mg

Conclusion

Thank you for making it to the end. The warning symptoms of diabetes type 1 are the same as type 2; however, in type 1, these signs and symptoms tend to occur slowly over a period of months or years, making it harder to spot and recognize. Some of these symptoms can even occur after the disease has progressed.

Each disorder has risk factors that when found in an individual, favor the development of the disease. Diabetes is no different. Here are some of the risk factors for developing diabetes.

Having a Family History of Diabetes

Usually having a family member, especially first-degree relatives could be an indicator that you are at risk of developing diabetes. Your risk of developing diabetes is about 15% if you have one parent with diabetes while it is 75% if both your parents have diabetes.

Having Prediabetes

Being pre-diabetic means that you have higher than normal blood glucose levels. However, they are not high enough to be diagnosed as type 2 diabetes. Having pre-diabetes is a risk factor for developing type 2 diabetes as well as other conditions such as cardiac conditions. Since there are no symptoms or signs for Prediabetes, it is often a latent condition that is discovered accidentally during routine investigations of blood glucose levels or when investigating other conditions.

Being Obese or Overweight

Your metabolism, fat stores and eating habits when you are overweight or above the healthy weight range contribute to abnormal metabolism pathways that put you at risk for developing diabetes type 2. There have been consistent research results of the obvious link between developing diabetes and being obese.

Having a Sedentary Lifestyle

Having a lifestyle where you are mostly physically inactive predisposes you to a lot of conditions including diabetes type 2. That is because being physically inactive causes you to develop obesity or become overweight. Moreover, you don't burn any excess sugars that you ingest which can lead you to become prediabetic and eventually diabetic.

Having Gestational Diabetes

Developing gestational diabetes which is diabetes that occurred due to pregnancy (and often disappears after pregnancy) is a risk factor for developing diabetes at some point.

Ethnicity

Belonging to certain ethnic groups such as Middle Eastern, South Asian or Indian background. Studies of statistics have revealed that the prevalence of diabetes type 2 in these ethnic groups is high. If you come from any of these ethnicities, this puts you at risk of developing diabetes type 2 yourself.

Having Hypertension

Studies have shown an association between having hypertension and having an increased risk of developing diabetes. If you have hypertension, you should not leave it uncontrolled.

Extremes of Age

Diabetes can occur at any age. However, being too young or too old means your body is not in its best form and therefore, this increases the risk of developing diabetes.

That sounds scary. However, diabetes only occurs with the presence of a combination of these risk factors. Most of the risk factors can be minimized by taking action. For example, developing a more active lifestyle, taking care of your habits and attempting to lower your blood glucose sugar by restricting your sugar intake. If you start to notice you are prediabetic or getting overweight, etc., there is always something you can do to modify the situation. Recent studies show that developing healthy eating habits and following diets that are low in carbs, losing excess weight and leading an active lifestyle can help to protect you from developing diabetes, especially diabetes type 2, by minimizing the risk factors of developing the disorder.

You can also have an oral glucose tolerance test in which you will have a fasting glucose test first and then you will be given a sugary drink and then having your blood glucose tested 2 hours after that to see how your body responds to glucose meals. In healthy individuals, blood glucose should drop again 2 hours post sugary meals due to the action of insulin.

Another indicative test is the HbA1C. This test reflects the average of your blood glucose level over the last 2 to 3 months. It is also a test to see how well you manage your diabetes.

People with diabetes type 1 require compulsory insulin shots to control their diabetes because they have no other option. People with diabetes type 2 can regulate their diabetes with healthy eating and regular physical activity although they may require some glucose-lowering medications that can be in tablet form or in the form of an injection.

All the above goes in the direction that you need to avoid a starchy diet because of its tendency to raise blood glucose levels. Too many carbohydrates can lead to insulin sensitivity and pancreatic fatigue, as well as weight gain with all its associated risk factors for cardiovascular disease and hypertension. The solution is to lower your sugar intake, therefore, decrease your body's need for insulin and increase the burning of fat in your body.

When your body is low on sugars, it will be forced to use a subsequent molecule to burn for energy, in that case, this will be fat. The burning of fat will lead you to lose weight.

I hope you have learned something!